EXTREME HABITATS

DESERTS

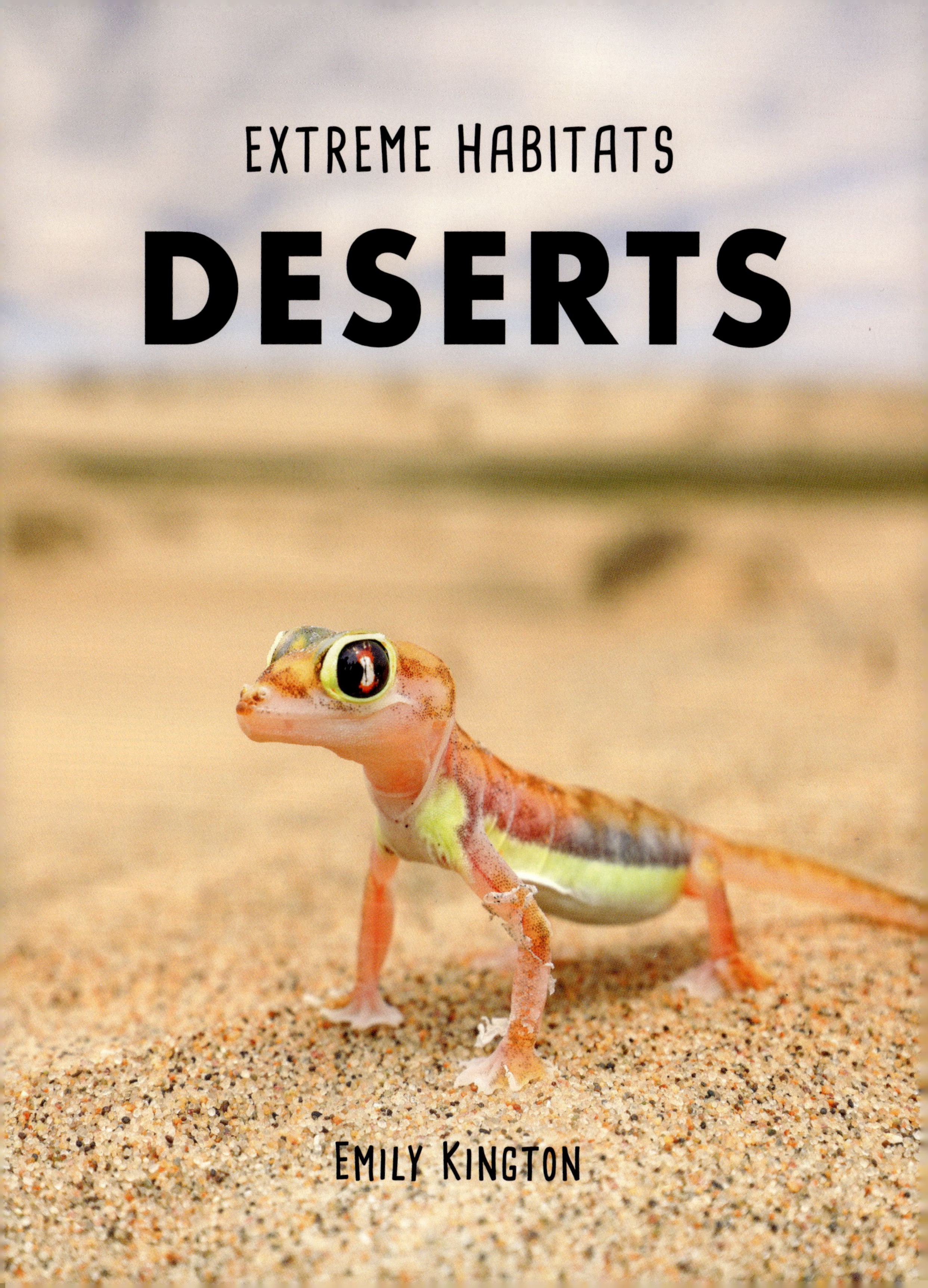

EMILY KINGTON

www.hungrytomato.com

Victoria House, Staplefield Lane,
Staplefield, West Sussex, UK

First published by
Hungry Tomato Ltd in 2021,
F1, Old Bakery Studios,
Blewetts Wharf, Malpas Road,
Truro, Cornwall, TR1 1QH, UK

ISBN 978 1 914087 073

Manufactured in the USA

A CIP catalogue record for this book is available from the British Library.

Picture credits

(t = top, b = bottom, l = left, r = right, m = middle, bg = background)

Corbis Hubert Stadler/Corbis 11b. Hugh Sitton/zefa/Corbis 27tr. Peter Lillie/ Gallo Images/Corbis 14r. Picture Library Ltd/Alamy 27br. Robert Cameron/ Getty 29tr. Shutterstock: 4b; 5mr; 7b; 8l; 8b; 9mr; 12b; 13mr; 16tr; 18bg; 20b; 21mr; 21b; 22br; 24b; 27mr; 27b; 28r; angkrit 13t; Ashley Whitworth 4tl; Bastien Schneider 6bg; Christoph Riddle 15mr; Denis Burdin 4bg; DnDavis 21br; EcoPrint 7mr; ene 19tl; GreenStockCreative 12tl; Jean Orrico 11mr; Jim Lopes 17tl; Johan Swanepoel 23br; Kertu 2bg; Kuttelvaserova Stuchelova 20tr; kyslynskahal 22tl; Lao Ma 17bg; Larsek 25mr; Lori Froeb 28br; Louie Schoeman 21tr; Lyle E. Doberstein 17mr; Martin Mecnarowski (front cover); Nathan Jaskowiak 16b; Ondrej Prosicky 1bg; Patrick Poendl 9b; Paul S. Wolf 25br; rangsan paidaen (fact file); R.M. Nunes 10bg; Rodney Mehring 13b; Sandra Caldwell 26bl; Sara Robinson 29mr; sinoptic (notebook and tips illustrations); sirtravelalot 6b; Steve Rosset 14bg; Triff 10tl; Uus Gumilar, Ugie 19mr; Vladimir Wrangel 9tl;

Every effort has been made to trace the copyright holders, and we apologise in advance for any unintentional omissions.We would be pleased to insert the appropriate acknowledgments in any subsequent edition of this publication.

CONTENTS

DRY, HOT AND EMPTY?

The red-barred dragon is a lizard found in some Australian deserts.

The ground under your feet is sandy and dry. There are no clouds in the sky and the Sun is burning hot. Not a sound can be heard and nothing moves. The desert all around you is lifeless... or is it?

Look closer, and you will find small **mammals** and lizards hidden in shady nooks. Under the ground, millions of plant seeds wait for the rains to fall.

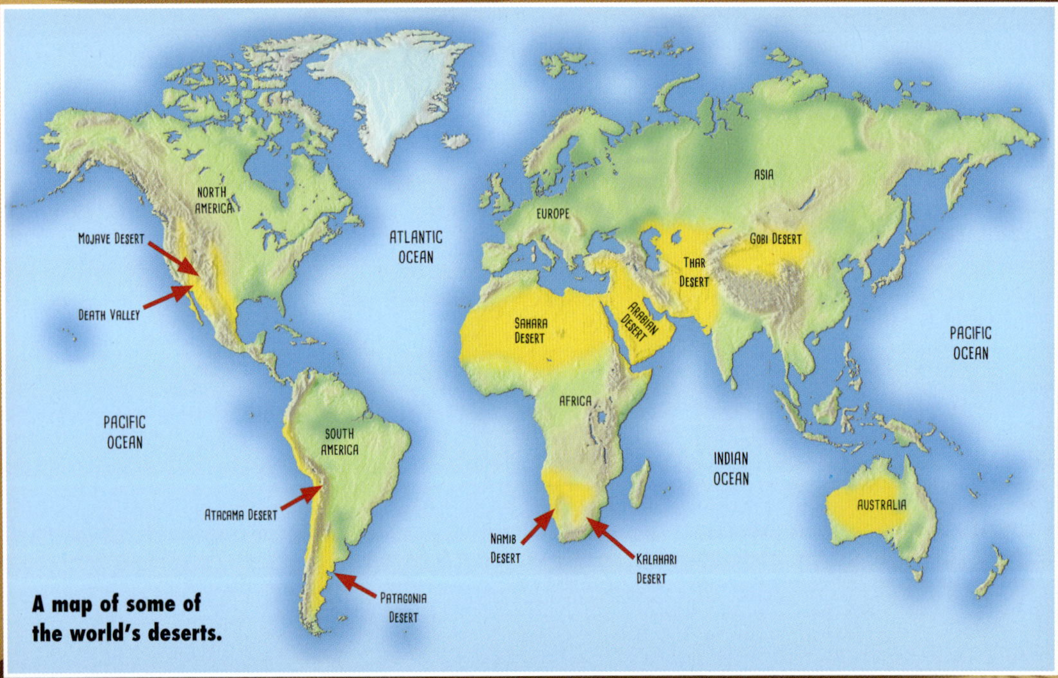

A map of some of the world's deserts.

In fact, thousands of animals and people live in deserts. Despite the heat, the lack of water and the blinding **sandstorms**, they survive. Could you?

A desert is a place where very little rain falls. Many deserts are also scorching hot, but not all. Some deserts, such as the **Gobi Desert** in Asia, can get very cold.

DESERT NOTEBOOK

- A desert is a place that gets less than 10 inches (25 centimeters) of rain or snow each year.
- Even if a desert is very hot in the day, it gets extremely cold at night.
- Sand covers only about 20 percent of Earth's deserts.

FENNEC FOX

- From space, deserts look empty and lifeless. But lots of different animals live in deserts. Many of them only come out at night, like the fennec fox.

DESERT SURVIVAL TIPS

Even if you don't feel thirsty, drink up! In a hot desert, an adult needs to drink 2-4 gallons (8-15 liters) of water every day.

JOURNEY INTO THE DESERT

White clothing reflects the sunlight and keeps the wearer cool.

Deserts are beautiful but deadly. In a hot desert, a healthy person left without water and shade in the morning could be dead by the evening.

Out of the shade, the hot Sun quickly burns your skin. The heat makes you sweat, so your body loses lots of water even when you are sitting in the shade.

If you are planning a trip into the desert, make sure you bring the right gear! The desert Sun is very harsh and will quickly burn bare skin. Sunblock, light clothes and wide-brimmed hats will keep the Sun off your body. At night it can get very cold, so you

Travel is difficult. Cars and trucks can get bogged down in the soft sand.

DESERT SURVIVAL TIPS

Getting lost in the desert is a fatal mistake. You are very unlikely to bump into anyone else! Use maps and compasses or satellite navigation to help you find your way.

will also need thick jackets and sleeping bags.

Bring water – lots of it! Many expeditions carry big water containers on trucks. If you do manage to find water, a **water filter** will make it safe to drink.

Be prepared for extreme weather such as sandstorms. Lightning can also be frequent in deserts, even if there is no rain.

DESERT NOTEBOOK

- Very few desert animals can kill a person, but spiders, scorpions and snakes can give you a nasty bite or sting

THE POISONOUS HORNED ADDER LIVES IN THE KALAHARI DESERT.

- More people drown in the Sahara Desert than die from thirst. That's because when it rains, dry valleys can turn into surging rivers in a few minutes.

Lightning strikes are so hot they can turn sand into glass. The sand forms a tube shape called a fulgurite.

THE LARGEST DESERT

The Sahara is by far the biggest hot desert in the world. It is about the same size as the United States, and stretches over 3,000 miles (5,000 km) from the Atlantic Ocean to the Red Sea. You would not want to get lost in a desert this size!

If you walked across the Sahara Desert, you would find many different landscapes. You would cross **sand dunes**, gravel plains and rocky uplands. In the middle of the desert, you'd climb tall mountains with snowy peaks.

The huge sand dunes of the Sahara are known as **ergs**. Sand dunes form where something, such as a plant, blocks the wind and sand builds up against it.

Camels are used to transport passengers and cargo in the Sahara Desert.

DESERT SURVIVAL TIPS

Some Saharan scorpions can kill a human with one sting from their tail. In the desert never put your hands or feet where your eyes can't see!

Ergs in the Sahara often form crescent shapes.

Desert peoples survive by wandering from one oasis to the next. An oasis is a green spot in a desert where plants can grow all year. The Sahara has 90 large oases where people live in villages and grow crops. But you can't always rely on an oasis – sometimes the water runs dry.

DESERT NOTEBOOK

- 8,000 years ago the Sahara was covered in grasslands and forests. Cave paintings from this time show giraffes, elephants, and crocodiles.

CAVE PAINTINGS IN THE SAHARA

- The Sahara is bigger than the next eight largest deserts put together.
- The world's highest sand dunes are in the north-east part of the Sahara. They are 1525 feet (465 meters) tall!

An oasis in the Sahara in Libya

THE ULTIMATE DUST BOWL

Nasa tests Mars Rovers in the Atacama Desert, its a good place to practice looking for life on Mars.

The Atacama Desert stretches along the coast of Chile, between the Pacific Ocean and the Andes Mountains. It is the driest desert in the world. In the very driest parts, scientists have found no signs of life. Even bacteria can't survive here.

The **Atacama Desert** is a **rain shadow desert**. A rain shadow desert forms when tall mountains block rain clouds from reaching the other side. The Andes Mountains block clouds blowing in from the east, and they release their rain before they can reach the Atacama Desert.

DESERT SURVIVAL TIPS

Heatstroke can cause vomiting, confusion and blackouts. Drink lots of water and seek shelter. Use the shade of your car if you have nothing else.

Only a few tough plants can survive in the Atacama Desert. They collect moisture from the **sea-fog** that rolls in from the Pacific Ocean. In many years, fog is the only water the desert gets.

Deserts are dry because the ground loses water faster than rain can keep the ground moist. Water drains away, or dries up and goes into the air as **water vapor**.

NASA scientists undertake Mars rover tests in the extreme dryness of the Atacama desert. They test Mars rovers ability to drive, drill and search for life.

This sandy, rocky landscape is typical of the Atacama Desert.

DESERT NOTEBOOK

- In parts of the Atacama Desert, no rainfall has ever been recorded.

A FLOCK OF FLAMINGOS

- Flocks of flamingos live around the Atacama salt lakes. They feed on red algae that grow in the waters. This gives them their pink color.

This modern concrete statue is 36 feet (11 meters) tall. It stands in the heart of the Atacama Desert, and many tourists go to see it every year.

HOT AS AN OVEN?

The Equator is an imaginary line around the center of the Earth.

Many of the world's deserts are found about 1860 miles (3,000 kilometers) north and south of the Equator. Here there are few clouds to shield the ground. The deserts are roasting hot in the day, and freezing cold at night.

Many deserts are not hot all year round. Their temperatures change with the seasons. A gentle hike through the Mojave Desert, in the USA, in January could turn into a fight for survival in July.

Some of the hottest temperatures ever recorded were in **Death Valley** in the Mojave Desert in 1917. For 43 days in a row, the maximum temperature was over 118°F (48°C).

The flat, empty desert allowed Thrust SSC to become the first car to break the sound barrier.

DESERT SURVIVAL TIPS

Is that a pool of water in the distance? Don't count on it! It may just be dry land. Mirages are tricks of the light, caused by sunlight on hot ground.

The smooth, flat surface of Black Rock Desert in Nevada, USA is perfect for land speed record attempts. In 1997, the Thrust SSC reached a record-breaking speed of 763 miles (1,228 kilometers) per hour.

DESERT NOTEBOOK

- The highest temperature ever recorded was in Death Valley, California, USA. On 10th July 1913, the thermometer reached a blistering 134.1°F (56.7°C).

SOME DESERTS ARE SO HOT THAT YOU COULD FRY EGGS ON THE ROCKS.

- The change from blazing heat during the day to freezing cold at night is enough to make rocks crack. Some split at night with a loud bang.

Lakes that have dried up leave behind a large area of flat land. They are ideal for breaking world speed records.

DESERT STORMS

Do you think deserts are still and peaceful? Think again. Deserts are among the windiest places on Earth. The blazing Sun bakes the ground and heats the air above it. The hot air rises, and cooler air rushes in to take its place. This creates wind – lots of it.

Grains of sand as seen under a microscope.

Fierce desert winds create amazing sculptures from rock. The sand wears away softer rock faster, leaving the harder rock standing.

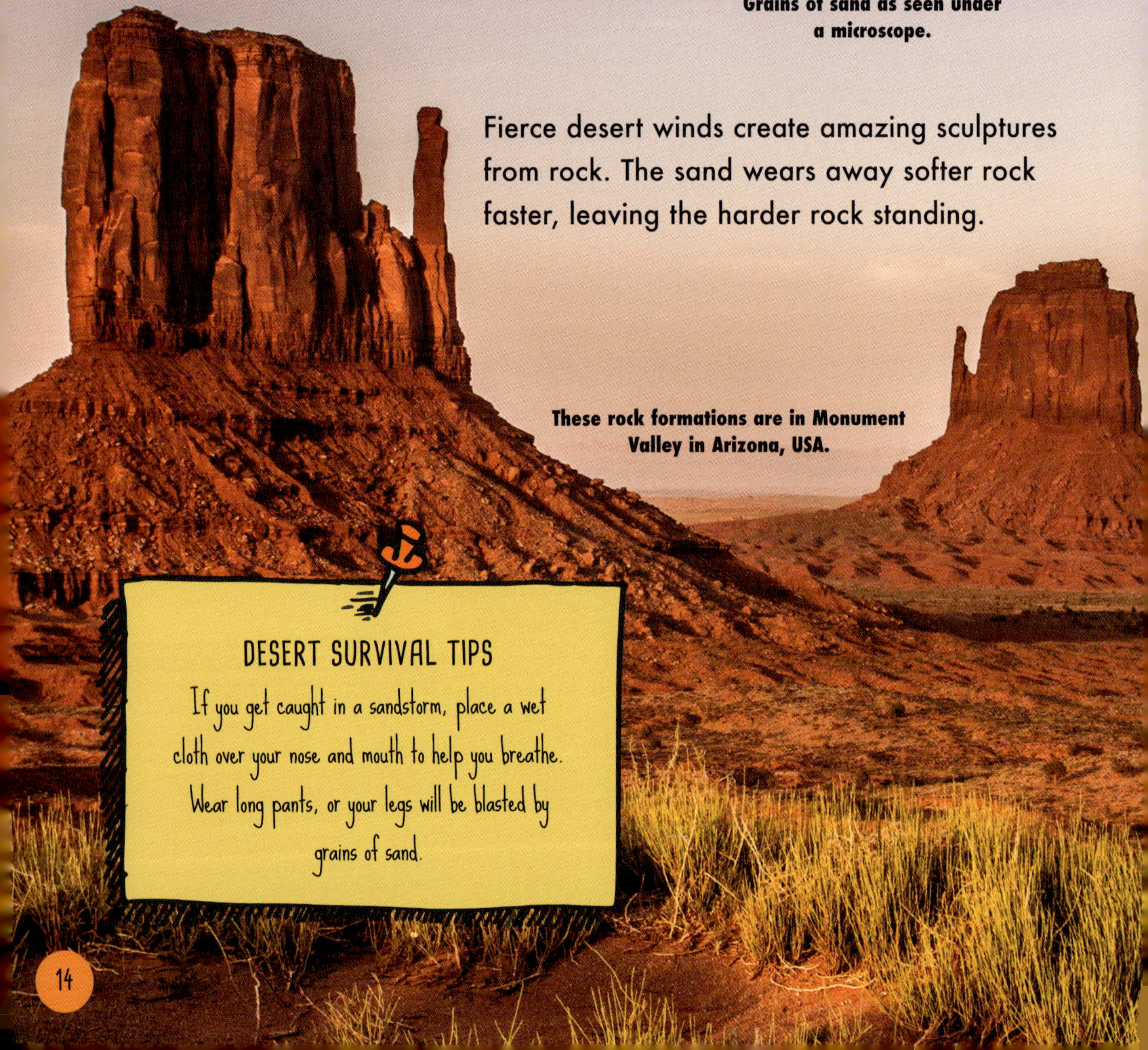

These rock formations are in Monument Valley in Arizona, USA.

DESERT SURVIVAL TIPS

If you get caught in a sandstorm, place a wet cloth over your nose and mouth to help you breathe. Wear long pants, or your legs will be blasted by grains of sand.

Sandstorms can leave a thick coating of dust and sand on plants, animals and houses.

The speed and direction of the winds change constantly. This creates arches and giant stacks of rock, as well as strange looking pillars and mushroom shapes called **hoodoos**.

DESERT NOTEBOOK

- Strong winds blow all year long in some parts of the Gobi Desert, pushing the sand along. Even the biggest sand dunes move about 160 feet (50 meters) a year.

TWO KITE BUGGIES RACE ACROSS THE DESERT.

- In 2006, 295,300 tons (300,000 metric tons) of sand were whipped up by a single sandstorm in the Gobi Desert. The storm dumped this sand on the city of Beijing, over 1,000 miles (1,600 km) away!

THE DEADLIEST DESERT

If you crossed the deadliest desert in the world you wouldn't have to worry about the heat! Antarctica has just 4 inches (10 centimeters) of snow each year, making Antarctica a desert. Antarctica is so dry that some parts are completely free of ice.

As well as being the coldest desert on Earth, **Antarctica** is also the windiest, highest, most isolated and least explored continent. If you want to explore an extreme habitat, look no further!

The **Dry Valleys** of Antarctica get almost no snowfall or moisture – they are even drier than the Sahara. The mountains block **glaciers** from moving into the valleys, leaving large areas of bare rock. Today, any moisture is soon sucked away by winds swooping down the valleys.

The Dry Valleys in Antarctica cover about 3,000 square miles (4,800 square kilometers).

The Gobi Desert is another cold desert. In winter, temperatures fall to -40°F (-40°C). In northwest China, there is a region of the Gobi Desert called the Takla Makan Desert, which means, "Go in and you won't come out again!"

DESERT SURVIVAL TIPS

The camels of the Gobi Desert can walk 31 miles (50 km) a day while carrying 300 lbs (140 kg) of cargo. Even today, camels move almost 30 percent of the cargo that passes across the Gobi Desert.

DESERT NOTEBOOK

- Some places in Antarctica haven't had any rain for four million years!
- In winter, temperatures in the Antarctic can fall to -126°F (-88°C), making it the coldest place on Earth.

SNOW LEOPARD

- The mountains of the Gobi Desert are home to the beautiful snow leopard, which hunts wild sheep, mountain goats and rabbits. Few people have ever seen this shy creature in the wild.
- There are cold deserts in many parts of the world. The Great Basin Desert in the western USA is a cold desert.

DESERT WONDERS

Minerals in the rock give the Vermillion Cliffs in Utah, USA their red color.

Even if you survive the heat, dust and wind of the desert, you might not get over its beauty! You can climb tall pillars of rock, explore deep canyons and walk across sand dunes shaped like crescents or stars.

Uluru, in the central desert of Australia, is the largest single rock in the world. It is about 1.2 miles (2 kilometers) long and 1.5 miles (2.5 kilometers) wide. At different times of the day, the rock appears to change color from blue, to violet, to glowing red. It is sacred to the local Anangu people, and ancient paintings decorate its cave walls.

A sunrise and sunset in the Painted Desert in Arizona, USA, the rocks and sand will shine in a rainbow of colors, from purple, to yellow, brown and red.

Uluru in Australia is made from a type of sandstone that makes it appear to glow at sunrise and sunset.

DESERT SURVIVAL TIPS

Avoid walking across a desert during the hottest hours of the day. Plane crash survivors have walked over 340 miles (550 kilometers) in 20 days by walking only at night.

El Tatio geysers in the Atacama Desert, in Chile.

Deserts are full of surprises. 14,100 feet (4,300 meters) up, in the Atacama Desert in Chile, are the amazing El Tatio **geysers**. These shoot pillars of water and steam, up to 16 feet (five meters) into the air. In the nearby hills is the 490 foot (150 meter) deep Chiu-Chiu Lagoon, a lake right in the middle of the desert.

DESERT NOTEBOOK

- Every year drivers race through the Sahara Desert during the Paris to Dakar rally. In 1983, 40 drivers had to be rescued after losing their way in a sandstorm.

A CAMEL RACE IN THE ARABIAN DESERT.

- Camels are also raced over the desert. Their top speed is over 18 miles (30 kilometers) per hour.

FACT FILE:

PLANT SURVIVORS

Only the toughest plants can live in a desert. Many are built to collect and store water. As a result, desert plants look unlike plants living in other habitats.

DESERT LOCUST

- Plants that store water often grow sharp spines to stop desert animals eating them.
- When there is a rain storm, seeds sprout, grow and bloom in just a few weeks. They can turn even a dry desert into a carpet of colorful flowers.
- When rain occurs in some dry areas of Africa and Asia, it can trigger a giant swarm of desert locusts.
- The swarm contains billions of locusts, and they eat everything in their path. Locust swarms can lead to **famine** for local people.

HOW DO CACTI SURVIVE IN THE DESERT?

Tough Plants

Welwitschia plant

Welwitschia plant

- This plant has leaves which grow up to 13 feet (4 meters) long. They collect water from nighttime sea-fog and send it to the plant's roots.
- It grows in the Namib Desert in Africa.
- Some plants may live for as long as 2,000 years.

Baobab tree

Baobab tree

- The tree has no leaves for most of the year.
- The leaves sprout only during the short rainy season.
- Its large trunk stores water for the nine dry months ahead. It is native to Africa and Australia.

Jumping cholla

Jumping cholla

- This cactus has stems that fall off so easily they seem to jump out and bite you when you pass by.
- This helps the cholla spread to new areas.
- The roots of a 3 foot (1 meter) tall cholla cover an area the size of a tennis court.

The Desert Paintbrush survives in the dry desert by taking water from the roots of neighboring plants.

FACT FILE

THE RED KANGAROO FROM AUSTRALIA CAN GO FOR MONTHS WITHOUT DRINKING AT ALL.

ANIMAL SURVIVORS

Desert animals need special bodies to cope with the dryness, the baking heat during the day and the bitter cold at night.

- Smaller animals survive by avoiding heat. The tiny elf owl shelters from the hot desert sunlight inside saguaro cacti.
- Larger animals survive by moving around, and will travel a long way from one **water hole** to the next.
- Many desert animals have pale colored skin, feathers or fur. This keeps them cool by reflecting sunlight. Light colors reflect the sun better than dark colors.
- Pale colors are also a good form of camouflage, helping the animals to blend in with the sand or rocks.

- Some animals avoid the hot Sun by going underground. The American spadefoot toad spends most of the year in a deep underground burrow. It only comes out to lay its eggs during the rainy season.

Spadefoot toad

HOW ARE PEOPLE AND CAMELS ADAPTED TO SURVIVE IN THE DESERT?

	Person	Camel
Days without water	1 day	20 days
Amount drunk in 10 minutes	4 pints (2 liters)	210 pints (120 liters)
Eyelashes (to prevent sand in eyes)	1 set	3 sets
Ability to walk on sand	Bad – *feet sink in sand.*	Good – *has tough soles and spreads its weight on four broad feet.*
Other adaptations	The ability to use tools and fire, and work in groups means that people can live comfortably in the desert.	Camels have a hump that stores fat for times when food is scarce. They also have a light colored coat to reflect the Sun and a tough mouth to eat spiny desert plants.

TRICKS FOR SURVIVAL

Jerboa

- Its long legs help it to move quickly over the hot desert sand.
- It gets its water from seeds, and so it does not need to drink.
- It does not sweat and it has very dry droppings.

Jerboa

Honeypot ants

- Honeypot ants gather nectar from flowers during the rainy season and feed it to special worker ants.
- These workers store the nectar in their bodies. During the dry summer season they spit out the nectar for the rest of the colony to feed on.

Honeypot ant

Sandgrouse

- A male sandgrouse will fly up to 100 miles (160 kilometers) a day to find water.
- It soaks up the water with its belly feathers. Then it flies home, bringing the water to its thirsty chicks.

Sandgrouse

THE GILA MONSTER IS THE LARGEST NORTH AMERICAN LIZARD.

DESERT HUNTERS

Even big hunters such as lions can survive in a desert. They get water from the blood of their prey. Many predators living in the desert hunt at night, keeping cool in rocky dens or burrows during the day.

- Some desert animals, like kingsnakes and geckos, have large eyes perfect for hunting at night.
- Other animals such as scorpions, use their senses of touch and smell to hunt in the dark.
- Many desert creatures, such as snakes, scorpions and spiders, have venomous bites or stings. Food is difficult to find in a desert, and venom stops their victims from running away!

A rattlesnake may rattle its tail to warn potential predators that it is venomous.

Desert food web

This diagram is a simple food web. It shows how desert predators rely on other animals for food. The red arrows point from the food to the animal that eats it.

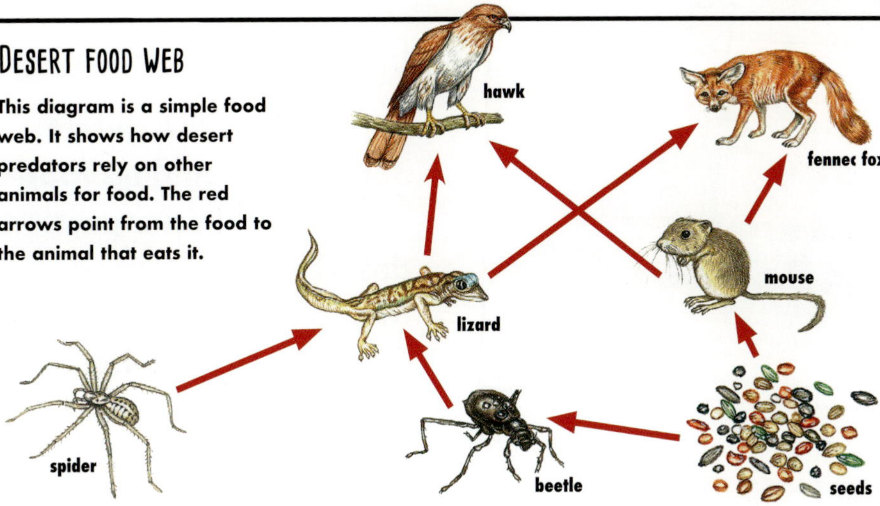

Clever Hunters

Vulture

Vulture

- Vultures escape the midday heat by soaring high into the cool air.
- They also cool their legs by peeing on them!

Sidewinder

Sidewinder snake

- This snake moves over the hot sand in a special way, so that only a small part of its body touches the hot sand at any time.
- It hunts by burying itself in sand and waiting for prey.

Roadrunner

Roadrunner

- A roadrunner can run at 16.5 miles (27 kilometers) per hour.
- This is quick enough to catch a rattlesnake. The roadrunner snaps up the snake by the tail and slams its head against the ground until it is dead.

Fennec fox

- A fennec fox's large ears help it listen out for prey when hunting at night.
- During the day, air passes over the fox's ears, which helps it to cool off.

FACT FILE

A YURT IS A TENT USED BY THE MONGOLS OF THE GOBI DESERT. THE YURT CAN BE EASILY MOVED, WHICH IS NECESSARY FOR A NOMADIC PEOPLE.

DESERT PEOPLE

Surviving in the desert depends on finding food and water. In the past, desert people stayed alive by moving from place to place. They camped wherever they stopped.

Witchetty grubs are sometimes eaten raw!

- Some desert people, such as the Bedouins and the Tuareg, are **herders** and **traders**.
- Camels, goats and sheep give **nomadic** people meat, milk, wool and skins.
- The San people are **hunters**. They live in family groups and hunt small mammals.
- Some Indigenous Australians are also hunters. They look for food such as wallabies, witchetty grubs, insects and berries.

This chart lists some groups of people who live in the world's major deserts.

Desert	People
Arabian	Bedouins
Australia	Indigenous Australians
Gobi	Mongols
Kalahari	San
Sahara	Tuareg

Wallabies are found throughout Australia.

Bedouin Survival Techniques

Headcloth

- This is wrapped around the head and often covers the neck as well.
- The headcloth is a shield from the Sun and provides protection against the cold.
- One end can be brought up to cover the nose and mouth, to keep the wind and sand out.

Bedouin headcloth

Tracking

- Tracking is a traditional skill, and was used to help the Bedouin hunt wild animals.
- A Bedouin may be able to spot the footprint of a relative as easily as you would recognise a friend's photo.

Footprint

Collecting water

- One Bedouin trick is to turn over half-buried stones in the desert just before the Sun rises. Fine drops of water form on the stones' cool surface.

Stone in the desert

An Indigenous Australian woman digs for grubs, which are a good source of protein.

FACT FILE

DESERT THREAT

The lack of water makes deserts unsuitable land for farming. Other land is also becoming unsuitable, mostly due to poor farming techniques. This increase in unuseable land is known as desertification.

- The areas around deserts are at risk of **desertification**. People must use the land carefully in order to farm there. Unfortunately, the people living near deserts are often poor, and they cut down trees for firewood. Without trees, there is little to stop the unproductive land from spreading.
- There are some positive developments that will slow the spread of deserts. Trees and tough grasses are being planted on the edges of deserts to stop them from spreading.
- In some areas, **canals** transfer water from lakes and rivers into desert areas.

Windmills like this are sometimes used to pump water in desert areas.

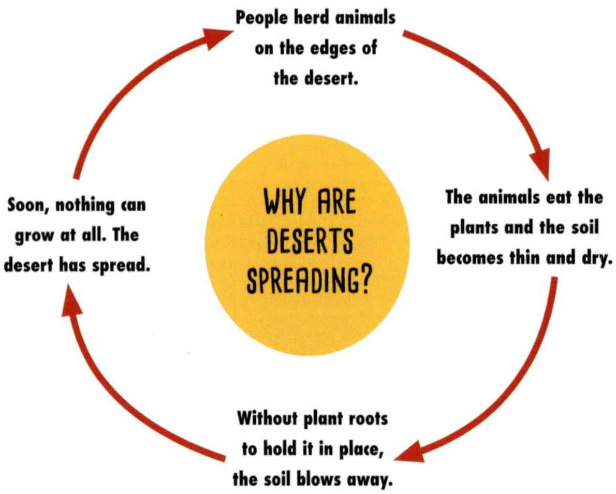

PLANT ROOTS HOLD SOIL IN PLACE.

Desert Problems

Groundwater
- Many people live in cities in desert areas, such as Las Vegas in the USA.
- Modern cities need lots of water.
- Machines pump water from deep underground up to the desert surface.
- This water may be used up faster than it can be replaced.

Roads
- Cities and busy roads make life difficult for big animals such as mountain lions.
- They need large wild areas to roam in, away from cars and humans.

Mining
- There are many riches in the desert, such as oil, minerals, gold and diamonds.
- Mining creates a lot of pollution.
- It also causes soil erosion, leading to desertification.

Las Vegas

Mountain lion

Mining

This map shows the areas around the Sahara Desert which are at risk of becoming deserts.

KEY
- Desert
- Severe risk
- Moderate risk

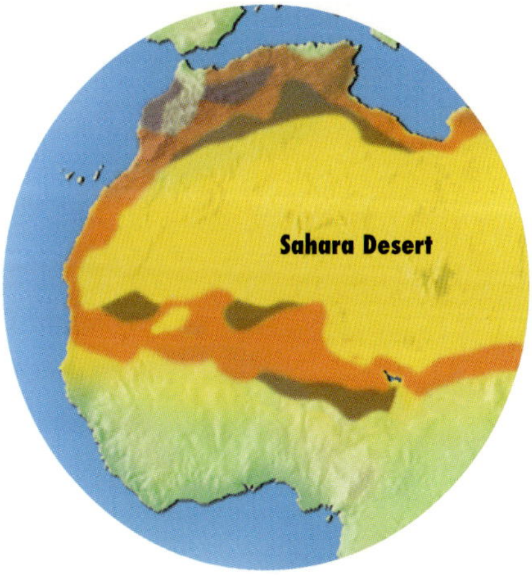

GLOSSARY

algae – simple plants which live in water, many of which can only be seen with a microscope.

Atacama Desert – a very dry desert in Chile, South America. It is long and narrow, about 90 miles (150 kilometers) wide and 600 miles (1,000 kilometers) long.

canals – waterways that are built to carry boats, or to take water from one place to another.

Death Valley – a very dry area in California in the USA, receiving less than 2 inches (5 centimeters) of rain a year. It is the site of the highest recorded temperature in the USA (56.7°C in 1913).

desertification – the way unproductive land is spreading because of human behavior.

drought – a long period of very little rain.

Dry Valleys – the area in Antarctica that is not covered with ice and snow.

Equator – the imaginary line drawn around the middle of the Earth. It divides the world into a southern half and a northern half.

erg – a large area of sand dunes.

famine – an extreme shortage of food.

fulgurite – glass-like shapes formed when lightning strikes sand.

geyser – a hot spring which shoots water and steam into the air.

glaciers – large masses of ice.

global warming – the gradual increase in the world's temperature.

Gobi Desert – a large cold desert covering parts of China and Mongolia, in Asia. Winter temperatures average -40°F (-40°C), while summer temperatures can reach 113°F (45°C).

herders – a group of people who keep herds of sheep, goats, horses or camels.

hoodoos – unusual shaped rocks, caused by the wind wearing away the soft parts of the rock.

mammals – animals with fur that give birth to live young and feed them on milk.

mirages – images of things (such as oases) that are not really there. They are caused when the heat bends the light rays from the Sun.

NASA – an organisation in the USA that sends astronauts into space.

nomadic – when a group of people do not settle in towns and villages, but instead move around searching for food for themselves or their herds of animals.

oasis (plural: oases) – a place in the desert where water is found.

rain shadow desert – a dry area found behind some mountains. If the winds blow from the same direction for most of the time, then the mountains block the rain clouds and very little rain reaches the area behind them.

Sahara Desert – the largest hot desert in the world. It is found in northern Africa. It covers over 3.5 million square miles (9 million square kilometers).

sand dunes – hills built of sand.

sandstorms – strong winds in a sandy desert. The wind picks the sand up and blows it around.

sea-fog – the fog that forms when the wet air above the sea cools and forms into water droplets and moves on shore.

soil erosion – the way the soil is washed away by rain or blown away by the wind.

traders – a group of nomads who make their living by buying and selling goods.

valleys – the low areas between cliffs or mountains.

water hole – a pool of water in a dry area.

water filter – a device for making water safe to drink. The filter catches the dirt, while tiny holes allow the water to trickle through.

water vapor – the tiny droplets of water in the air after water has evaporated.

INDEX